THE DAWN OF PLANET EARTH

The incredible
story of
life on Earth

4,540 to 200 million years ago

Thanks to the creative team:
Senior Editor: Alice Peebles
Designer: Lauren Woods and collaborate agency
Consultant: Paolo Viscardi

First American edition published in 2015 by Lerner Publishing Group, Inc.

First published in Great Britain in 2015 by Hungry Tomato Ltd.

Hungry Tomato™
A division of Lerner Publishing Group, Inc.
241 First Avenue North
Minneapolis, MN 55401 USA

For reading levels and more information, look up this title at
www.lernerbooks.com.

Main body text set in Burbank Big Regular Medium.
Typeface provided by House Industries.

Library of Congress Cataloging-in-Publication Data

Rake, Matthew, author.
   The dawn of planet Earth / by Matthew Rake ; Illustrated by Peter Minister.
      pages cm. – (Field guide to evolution)
   "Original Edition Copyright © 2015 Hungry Tomato Ltd."
   Audience: Ages 8-12
   Audience: Grades 4 to 6
   ISBN 978-1-4677-6348-6 (lb : alk. paper) – ISBN 978-1-4677-7193-1 (pb : alk. paper) – ISBN 978-1-4677-7194-8 (eb pdf)
   1. Evolution (Biology)–Juvenile literature. 2. Paleontology–Juvenile literature. 3. Animals, Fossil–Juvenile literature. 4. Life (Biology)–Juvenile literature. I. Minister, Peter, illustrator. II. Title.
QH367.1.R27 2016
576.8–dc23   2015002508

Manufactured in the United States of America
1 - VP - 7/15/15

THE DAWN OF PLANET EARTH

By Matthew Rake

Illustrated by Peter Minister

HUNGRY
TOMATO™

Everything alive
today is related to
life from the past.

CONTENTS

* mya *means "million years ago"*

Hi. My name is Ackerley. I'm an Acanthostega.

I'm your guide. I've got the world's greatest story to tell you: how life evolved on Earth. Or to put it another way...

...how we all got here.

The story of prehistoric Earth is the story of how tiny microorganisms, so small you can't see them, evolved into huge dinosaurs. It's also the story of how your kind, *Homo sapiens,* came into being.

But I'm getting ahead of myself.

You humans have only been around for about 200,000 years, but the world is 4,500 million years (which is the same as 4.5 billion years) old.

If I made a 24-hour clock of the Earth's history, with the formation of the planet at midnight, the first life would appear around 4:00 a.m., the first animals with skeletons just after 8:00 p.m., the first dinosaurs at 10:45 p.m., and the first cat around 11:50 p.m. When would you *Homo sapiens* arrive? About three seconds to midnight. That's in the very last seconds of the very last minute of the very last hour.

So it's a big story. In this book, we'll see how the world was formed and how the first microorganisms came into being.

Then I'll show you some of the first animals, including this little creature. And, yes, that is a claw at the end of its trunk.

How do we know this stuff?

Scientists who study the history of living things are known as paleontologists. To learn about life in the past, they find and study fossils. Fossils are simply the remains of animals and plants that have been preserved in rocks.

There are two types of fossil: body fossils and trace fossils. A body fossil preserves the actual parts of an animal or plant. A trace fossil preserves the marks that organisms have made. For example, an animal may have made a burrow or footprints, or a plant may have left holes where its roots once were.

I'll also tell you about some of the scariest creatures, including the giant sea scorpion, a predator that grew bigger than one of you *Homo sapiens* and had claws the size of tennis rackets.

The first land animal we know of was a tiny millipede. Around 100 million years later, millipedes were growing to the size of crocodiles.

Invertebrates weren't the only animals on the land. Fish started to develop lungs and legs so they could live on land.

This is where I come in.

You see, we Acanthostegas have a big claim to fame: we were one of the first species to climb out of the water onto land.

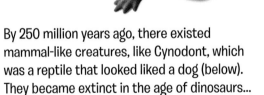

By 250 million years ago, there existed mammal-like creatures, like Cynodont, which was a reptile that looked liked a dog (below). They became extinct in the age of dinosaurs...

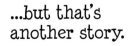

...but that's another story.

Changing Shape of the Planet

You may think the map of the world has always looked the same. But the continents have changed dramatically throughout the history of Earth, just as animals and plants have.

About 225 million years ago, the whole world was one big supercontinent called Pangea.

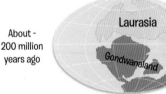

About -
225 million
years ago

About 200 million years ago, the continent of Pangea was dividing into Laurasia in the north and Gondwanaland in the south.

Laurasia

About -
200 million
years ago

Gondwanaland

By 65 million years ago, when the dinosaurs were wiped out, the world was looking much more like it does today. Laurasia was splitting up into North America in the west and Europe and Asia in the east. Gondwanaland had split into South America, Africa, India, and Antarctica/Australia.

About -
65 million
years ago

In the last 65 million years, North and South America have joined up, Antarctica and Australia separated, and India merged with the continent of Asia.

EVOLUTION TIMELINE

The story begins with the Big Bang 15,000 million years ago (mya). Life on Earth starts around 3,800 mya. Oxygen forms in the atmosphere about 2,300 mya as a waste product of photosynthesizing bacteria, in what the scientists call the Great Oxygenation Event. The ozone layer begins forming in Earth's atmosphere 600 mya. This will eventually protect Earth from the harmful rays of the sun. These events mean that animals will eventually be able to live on the land.

The first reptiles evolve from one branch of amphibians. Reptiles are the first animals with backbones to live permanently on land. Vast forests cover the land, and these will eventually fossilize to become coal.

Sea animals start appearing in the "Cambrian explosion of life" 540-520 mya. They swim, crawl, burrow, hunt, defend themselves, and hide away. Some creatures evolve hard parts such as shells.

Life begins on land as plants grow by lakes, streams, and coasts, and arthropods (animals with segmented bodies like millipedes) venture onto land. The first jawed fish appear.

Precambrian

Cambrian

Devonian

Carboniferous

Precambrian 4,540-541 mya	Cambrian 541-485 mya	Ordovician 485-443 mya	Silurian 443-419 mya	Devonian 419-359 mya	Carboniferous 359-299 mya

The "golden age of the dinosaurs" witnesses huge herbivore dinosaurs feeding on lush ferns and palm-like cycads. Smaller but vicious meat-eating dinosaurs hunt the great herbivores.

Homo sapiens appear in Africa around 200,000 years ago. By 40,000 years ago, they are also living in Europe, southern Asia and Australia. Around 16,000 years ago, they move into North America.

Dinosaurs appear, as do the first mammals and the first flying animals with backbones, the pterosaurs.

Many different mammals evolve. Some stay on land. Some, like whales, go back into the water. Some, like monkeys, take to the trees.

Triassic

Jurassic

Cretaceous

Paleogene

Neogene

Quaternary

Permian 299-252 mya	Triassic 252-201 mya	Jurassic 201-145 mya	Cretaceous 145-66 mya	Paleogene 66-23 mya	Neogene 23-2.6 mya	Quaternary 2.6 mya - now

BIRTH OF THE EARTH

For millions of years, there was no life on the planet.

In fact, to begin with, there was no planet at all!

Earth started off simply as dust and gas, spinning in a spiral. Gradually, it gathered more rocks from space, like a whirlpool funneling more and more material into its center.

With gravity pulling everything together, Earth eventually became a solid planet: a great ball of molten rock and metal with a solid outer crust.

When Earth first formed 4,540 million years ago, it was not exactly a great place for life. There was no water, no breathable air, and no protection from the rays of the sun. From the inside of the planet, red-hot liquid rock, known as lava, spewed out in huge volcanic eruptions. From the outside, fiery meteorites bombarded the surface.

For life to begin, Earth needed water. Today, water covers 70% of the planet. But where did it all come from?

Scientists once believed that since Earth was so hot, water must have come from outside the planet. Perhaps a comet, packed with ice, crashed into Earth. However, we can now analyze water evaporating off comets, and it's different from Earth's water.

Many modern scientists think that water was actually trapped deep inside the planet and forced out as steam in the volcanic eruptions. Eventually, when Earth cooled, the steam turned to liquid water.

Did You Know?

Because the world was full of fire and molten rock for the first 500 million years, scientists named this period the Hadean eon after the Greek god of the underworld, Hades.

Earth's oldest known rocks are from the Hadean eon. They come from Jack Hill in Western Australia and are 4,400 million years old.

HELL AND HIGH WATER

So how did this horribly hot and violent world change into the planet that we know, with forests, rivers, and oceans bursting with all kinds of life? Well, the volcanoes created great clouds of steam. That steam collected in a thick blanket around the whole world.

And then it rained.

And when I say rain, I mean rain: a deluge that went on for thousands, perhaps even millions, of years! Think about that the next time you complain about getting caught in a passing shower.

All living things are made up of cells, the basic building blocks of life, and the first living things were composed of just one cell each. They are known as microorganisms.

Scientists can't agree on exactly where the first microorganisms formed. Some think it was in shallow pools of seawater, some say in water droplets in the air. But the most recent theory is that life started at the bottom of the ocean, where boiling water shot up through vents from Earth's center.

It doesn't sound a prime spot for life to exist, hundreds of feet down where no sunlight ever reaches. But the hot water bursting upward would have carried minerals and energy to help. And anyway, Earth's surface was being bombarded by meteorites and covered with volcanic lava.

Today, we know that whole communities of living things, including microorganisms, worms, and giant clams, collect around the hot water of deep-sea vents.

Did You Know?

Many of the first microorganisms, such as algae, became trapped in multiple layers of rock, known as stromatolites. In Australia, scientists have found stromatolites containing algae fossils from 3,500 million years ago. So you can actually see evidence of some of the first living things ever to appear on Earth.

A SEA CHANGE

If there were a prize for The Weirdest Creature That Ever Lived, **Opabinia** would be a hot favorite for the top spot. It had five mushroom-shaped eyes, 15 segments on its body, and a grasping claw at the end of a long nose (or proboscis, to give it its scientific name). This animal used its extra proboscis to feed itself, much like an elephant uses its trunk. Perhaps it could even pull worms out of holes with its claw.

Opabinia

Another contestant for The Weirdest Creature That Ever Lived would definitely be **Hallucigenia** (right). When it was first studied in the 1970s, scientists thought it walked along the bottom of the seafloor on spiny stilts and that waving tentacles grew on its back. But now experts think the tentacles were actually legs and the spines on its back provided protection. Turning it upside down might make more sense, but it still looks pretty strange!

It took about 3,000 million years for life to evolve from simple cells into soft-bodied sea animals.

That's about two-thirds of the whole age of the planet!

And what a strange-looking bunch of animals they were, when they finally did appear...

Hallucigenia

Precambrian
4,540-541 mya

**Cambrian
541-485 mya**

Ordovician
485-443 mya

Silurian
443-419 mya

Devonian
419-359 mya

Carboniferous
359-299 mya

Permian
299-252 mya

Triassic
252-201 mya

Jurassic
201-145 mya

Cretaceous
145-66 mya

Paleogene
66-23 mya

Neogene
23-2.6 mya

Quaternary
2.6 mya - present

Did You Know?

Many of the best-preserved fossils of early animals come from Burgess Shale in the Rocky Mountains in Canada. In some fossils, you can even see the food the animal last ate inside its body...and it's over 500 million years old!

15

SLAYERS IN THE SEA

Soon some creatures started hunting and eating each other in the seas. They are known as predators, and many of them have survived all the way to your time.

Some, I must say, look distinctly unfriendly...

Nautiloid

Another fast and fearsome predator was the **nautiloid**. It lived inside a shell and chased prey by jet propulsion (spewing water from its body with enough force to push itself forward). Once the nautiloid had caught up with its unfortunate victim, it would pull the prey into its mouth using its cluster of grasping tentacles. One type of nautiloid, Endoceras, grew up to 11 feet (3.5 m) long. That's the length of a mini car!

Around 470 million years ago, the most fearsome killer was the **sea scorpion**. It could grow longer than a human and move quickly and nimbly through the water with the help of its long paddles. Then there were its deadly gripping claws: they were the size of tennis rackets and could hold prey against the sea floor before slicing and dicing!

SEA SCORPION (Eurypterid)
Location: Worldwide
Length: up to 8 feet (2.5m)

| Precambrian 4,540-541 mya |
| **Cambrian 541-485 mya** |
| **Ordovician 485-443 mya** |
| Silurian 443-419 mya |
| Devonian 419-359 mya |
| Carboniferous 359-299 mya |
| Permian 299-252 mya |
| Triassic 252-201 mya |
| Jurassic 201-145 mya |
| Cretaceous 145-66 mya |
| Paleogene 66-23 mya |
| Neogene 23-2.6 mya |
| Quaternary 2.6 mya - present |

Sea scorpion

Did You Know?

A handful of nautiloid species exist today around Australia and the Philippines. Other sea animals that have survived from 475 million years ago include coral and sea lilies. Coral are tiny sack-like creatures that use tentacles to sweep up food.

MONSTER OF THE DEEP

The first fish emerged around 510 million years ago. They were jawless and looked like giant tadpoles. They wriggled slowly along the seabed with their mouths open, sucking up tiny animals. Over millions of years, though, they developed jaws to bite with, forked tail fins to turn quickly, and bony heads for protection against predators, such as the sea scorpion (see previous page).

One of these bony-headed fish was the 9,000-pound (4-ton) monster, **Dunkleosteus**. It had an armor-plated skull about 4 feet (1.3 meters) wide. The plating itself was as much as 2 inches (5 centimeters) thick, and the sharpened edges of this plating served as teeth.

What's more, Dunkleosteus had some bite. Its force has been estimated at 1,100 pounds (5,000 N). That's more powerful than the bite of today's lions, tigers, or hyenas. Dunkleosteus could also open its mouth very quickly, in just one-fiftieth of a second, which created a strong suction force, pulling fast-moving prey into its mouth.

WOW, look at this guy! Pretty scary, huh?

I'm a bit worried. This monstrosity lived at the same time as I did, and I'd fit straight into that mouth. No wonder my ancestors adapted to escape onto land!

Dunkleosteus

Dunkleosteus did not have teeth. Instead it ate with the sharpened edges of bony plates around its head. These plates continued to grow as they were worn down by use. And as the top and bottom plates rubbed against each other, they were always kept sharp.

DUNKLEOSTEUS
Location: Worldwide
Length: 20 feet (6m)

Precambrian	4,540-541 mya
Cambrian	541-485 mya
Ordovician	485-443 mya
Silurian	443-419 mya
Devonian	419-359 mya
Carboniferous	359-299 mya
Permian	299-252 mya
Triassic	252-201 mya
Jurassic	201-145 mya
Cretaceous	145-66 mya
Paleogene	66-23 mya
Neogene	23-2.6 mya
Quaternary	2.6 mya - present

Did You Know?

Often a Dunkleosteus skeleton has scars that were caused by the jaws of another Dunkleosteus, showing that this killer did not fear attacking its own kind!

19

FISH WITH FINGERS

Recognize this good-looking guy?

Yes, it's me, hanging with some of my friends down by the riverbank. We were one of the first species to develop legs. This allowed us to climb out of the water onto land.

Acanthostega

Scientists don't think an Acanthostega's legs could have supported its body weight, so they believe it developed them (and its fingers) to move around shallow waters filled with plants and other debris.

So why did some fish decide that life would be better on land than in water? During the Devonian period, the Earth became warmer and drier. This meant lakes and rivers became shallower, with less oxygen and food for the animals that lived under the surface.

Some fish, known as the "fleshy fins" or "lobe fins," had lungs as well as gills, so they could breathe oxygen from the air. They developed muscular fins to pull themselves through shallow waters and to new pools. After many generations, these fins turned into limbs.

Precambrian 4,540-541 mya	
Cambrian 541-485 mya	
Ordovician 485-443 mya	
Silurian 443-419 mya	
Devonian 419-359 mya	
Carboniferous 359-299 mya	
Permian 299-252 mya	
Triassic 252-201 mya	
Jurassic 201-145 mya	
Cretaceous 145-66 mya	
Paleogene 66-23 mya	
Neogene 23-2.6 mya	
Quaternary 2.6 mya - present	

One of the first animals to do this was **Acanthostega**. It evolved limbs and digits but not ankles and knees strong enough to support the weight of its body, so walking on land would probably have been extremely difficult!

Slightly more successful was **Ichthyostega**, which lived at the same time as Acanthostega. It hauled itself from the water using its front limbs as crutches, the way a seal moves on the land today.

Did You Know?

Acanthostega and Ichthyostega were the first known tetrapods (animals with four feet). They are the ancestors of all the first four-limbed animals with backbones.

THE PROMISED LAND

For over 3,000 million years, all life on Earth existed in water. Creatures could not survive on land because of the harmful ultraviolet rays of the sun. However, algae in the water produced oxygen, and this eventually created a protective ozone layer around the Earth.

Then plants and arthropods (animals with jointed legs) became adapted to live on land.

Now this story has some legs...

Millipedes thrived in the Carboniferous period, when Earth had plenty of oxygen in the atmosphere and few large predators. In some cases, the millipedes grew very, very large. **Arthropleura** became the size of a modern-day crocodile!

Around 440 million years ago, plants appeared on land for the first time. These were mosses and liverworts that grew flat along the ground. **Cooksonia** was the first plant that stood upright, with roots to take in water and tubes to carry the water to the stems.

Once plants were growing on land, they provided a food source and shelter for animals. The oldest known land animal is **Pneumodesmus** (pronounced new-mo-des-mus), a millipede that lived 428 million years ago.

Arthropleura

ARTHROPLEURA
Location: America, Scotland
Length: Up to 8.5 feet (2.6m)

Precambrian	4,540-541 mya
Cambrian	541-485 mya
Ordovician	485-443 mya
Silurian	**443-419 mya**
Devonian	**419-359 mya**
Carboniferous	**359-299 mya**
Permian	299-252 mya
Triassic	252-201 mya
Jurassic	201-145 mya
Cretaceous	145-66 mya
Paleogene	66-23 mya
Neogene	23-2.6 mya
Quaternary	2.6 mya - present

The only known fossil of Pneumodesmus was found by Mike Newman, a bus driver from Scotland. He discovered it at the seaside town of Stonehaven. "I basically stood on it," he said. The creature was given the full name of *Pneumodesmus newmani* in Newman's honor.

The fossil is only 0.5 inch (1 cm) long, but it is detailed enough to show spiracles: tiny holes for taking in oxygen. This proves the millipede lived on land because the spiracles would have filled up with water in rivers.

RISE OF THE REPTILES

He might look as big and ferocious as many dinosaurs, but Dimetrodon was actually a reptile that evolved from early tetrapods living about 50 million years before the dinosaurs. In fact, he was more like you mammals than a dinosaur. Here he seems to have a taste for tetrapods like me.

Thank goodness he isn't around in my era

...but 70 million years later!

Reptiles were the first animals with backbones (vertebrates) able to live on land all the time. They developed scales to stop them from losing water through their skin and strong legs to help them move around easily.

Dimetrodon

The first reptile was **Hylonomus**. It lived 312 million years ago and was only 18 inches (20 cm) long, including the tail. **Dimetrodon** lived about 30 million years later and was about 15 times as long, making it a fearsome predator.

People have debated why Dimetrodon had a "sail" on its back. They once thought it might have been for camouflage among reeds while it waited for its prey, or to use like an actual boat sail to catch the wind while it was in the water!

Many experts think the sail might have controlled Dimetrodon's body temperature. Cold-blooded reptiles need to warm up in the morning, so maybe the sail helped to soak up sunshine. Or perhaps, like the peacock's tail, it was a way of attracting mates.

Dimetrodon means "two shapes of teeth" in Greek. At the front of this creature's mouth were stabbing canines ideal for piercing skin. At the back, its shearing teeth sliced up bone and tough muscle. These teeth curved backward so prey would be trapped in Dimetrodon's mouth. The surface of each tooth was serrated like the edge of a steak knife.

DIMETRODON
Location: America and Europe
Length: About 11 feet (3m)

| Precambrian 4,540-541 mya |
| Cambrian 541-485 mya |
| Ordovician 485-443 mya |
| Silurian 443-419 mya |
| Devonian 419-359 mya |
| **Carboniferous 359-299 mya** |
| **Permian 299-252 mya** |
| Triassic 252-201 mya |
| Jurassic 201-145 mya |
| Cretaceous 145-66 mya |
| Paleogene 66-23 mya |
| Neogene 23-2.6 mya |
| Quaternary 2.6 mya - present |

Did You Know?

Reptiles like Dimetrodon laid their eggs on dry land, not in water like earlier tetrapods. Inside each shell, a waterproof covering, called an amnion, protected the baby and stopped it from drying out.

HUNTING IN PACKS

Moschops was a reptile that did not look quite right. Its big, barrel-shaped body seems too large for its short legs, tiny feet, and little tail. However, being close to the ground meant it could graze on low-lying vegetation. And its sturdy build had another advantage: helping it withstand attacks, perhaps from a pack of **cynodonts**.

Moschops

Cynodont ("dog teeth") was a name for a huge variety of creatures. Some were carnivores, some herbivores. Some were the size of modern domestic cats, some as large as wolves.

The carnivorous cynodont was a fast and fierce creature. It had pointed canine teeth that could tear off chunks off flesh. Since mammals have similar teeth, scientists believe cynodonts were one of the first steps toward the evolution of mammals. Cynodonts also had powerful legs under their bodies like mammals, rather than at the sides like most reptiles.

Cynodont

Moschops looks as if it should have been able to protect itself. It was bigger than a hippo and had a strong, hard head. In fact, I'm told these guys would head-butt each other to show their dominance. Well, it looks as if this particular Moschops might want to try

head-butting some of those cynodonts...

MOSCHOPS
Location: South African forests
Length: About 16 feet (5m)

| Precambrian 4,540-541 mya |
| Cambrian 541-485 mya |
| Ordovician 485-443 mya |
| Silurian 443-419 mya |
| Devonian 419-359 mya |
| Carboniferous 359-299 mya |
| **Permian 299-252 mya** |
| Triassic 252-201 mya |
| Jurassic 201-145 mya |
| Cretaceous 145-66 mya |
| Paleogene 66-23 mya |
| Neogene 23-2.6 mya |
| Quaternary 2.6 mya - present |

Did You Know?

During the "Great Dying," the Permo-Triassic mass extinction 252 mya, 95% of all marine species became extinct. This enabled reptiles to rule the planet.

MEET THE MAMMALS

There were all kinds of creatures around in the Triassic period. Take this guy: he might not look like it, but he's actually a reptile. And just to confuse matters more, he has a beak like a Ceratopsia dinosaur. The other little critters might look more familiar to you.

They are your ancestors.

These were some of Earth's first mammals.

Megazostrodon

Although the Triassic period is known as the time when dinosaurs rose to dominance, it also saw the first mammals appear. Mammals suckle their young with milk, have hair or fur, and are warm-blooded.

Scientists think little shrew-like **Megazostrodon**, which appeared about 210 million years ago, may have been one of the first mammals. They believe it probably suckled its young after they hatched. Of course, scientists can't be sure, because fossils do not tell us much about how the young fed, or whether an animal had fur or was warm-blooded.

You might think **Hyperodapedon** would fancy one of those Megazostrodons for lunch, especially given its fearsome beak. In fact, Hyperodapedon used it to break open the seeds of now-extinct plants called seed ferns. Once the seed husk was split open, the animal chewed the softer insides at the back of its mouth so it could digest them easily.

MEGAZOSTRODON
Location: South African woods
Length: 4-5 inches (10-12cm)

| Precambrian |
| 4,540-541 mya |
| Cambrian |
| 541-485 mya |
| Ordovician |
| 485-443 mya |
| Silurian |
| 443-419 mya |
| Devonian |
| 419-359 mya |
| Carboniferous |
| 359-299 mya |
| Permian |
| 299-252 mya |
| **Triassic** |
| **252-201 mya** |
| Jurassic |
| 201-145 mya |
| Cretaceous |
| 145-66 mya |
| Paleogene |
| 66-23 mya |
| Neogene |
| 23-2.6 mya |
| Quaternary |
| 2.6 mya - present |

Hyperodapedon

Not many animals fed on seed ferns, so Hyperodapedon did not have to compete with other herbivores for food supplies. But when seed ferns disappeared at the end of the Triassic period, so did Hyperodapedon.

Hallucigenia

Pronounced: hal-loo-si-gen-ia

For a long time, Hallucigenia was thought to be an "evolutionary misfit": not related to any other animals alive. But in 2014, scientists suggested it was related to modern velvet worms, which live in tropical forests.

Sea scorpion (or Eurypterid)

Pronounced: your-rip-ter-rid

The sea scorpion's claws were equiped with long sharp spines that could have grasped even a slippery fish. They were probably designed for shooting out when close to prey, like the arms of a praying mantis.

Nautiloid

Pronounced: nawt-ill-oid

Today's nautiloids are sometimes called "living fossils" because they have changed very little over millions of years. However, only nautiloids with curved shells, not straight ones (as on page 16), have survived.

Dunkleosteus

Pronounced: dun-kul-oss-tee-us

Dunkleosteus was a type of fish known as a placoderm, which literally means "plated skin." Placoderms lasted about 50 million years. Sharks appeared at about the same time, but they have survived for over 400 million years.

Arthropleura

Pronounced: ar-thro-plur-ah

Fossil hunters have found fossilized footprints of Arthropleura, as well as fossilized body parts. They show that the giant millipede moved quickly across forest floors, swerving to avoid obstacles, such as trees and rocks.

Dimetrodon

Pronounced: die-met-roe-don

Twenty species of Dimetrodon have been found, the first one in 1878. The latest discovery is *Dimetrodon teutonis*. It was found in 2001 in Germany.

Moschops

Pronounced: mo-shops

It wasn't just the barrel-shaped body that made this creature look bizarre. Its front legs were longer than its hind legs, and they sprawled outward, like a lizard's, while the hind legs were directly under the body, like a mammal's.

Cynodont

Pronounced: sigh-no-dont

Cynodonts had teeth like mammals: they had incisors at the front, canines at the sides, and molars at the back. This is one reason why scientists think they may have been an ancestor of mammals.

Hyperodapedon

Prounounced: high-per-oh-dap-eh-don

Hyperodapedon fossils have been found all over the area that used to be the supercontinent Pangea. This herbivore reptile was probably a primary food source for late Triassic predators such as Saurosuchus.

Megazostrodon

Pronounced: meg-ah-zo-stroh-don

Megazostrodon evolved from cynodonts. Experts believe the creature was the last step between "mammal-like" reptiles such as cynodonts and true mammals. Like mammals, Megazostrodon was warm-blooded.

INDEX

THE AUTHOR

Matthew Rake lives in London and has worked in publishing for more than 20 years. He has written on a wide variety of topics, including science, sports, and the arts.

THE ARTIST

Peter Minister started out as a special-effects sculptor and had a successful and exciting career producing sculptures and props for museums, theme parks, TV, and film. He now works in CGI, which allows him to express himself with a big ball of digital clay in a more creative way than any "real" clay. His CGI dinosaurs and other animals have appeared in numerous books worldwide.